W9-BIZ-101

The
Death *of*
Common
Sense

The
Death *of*
Common
Sense

And profiles of those who knew him

Lori Borgman

Also by Lori Borgman

I WAS A BETTER MOTHER BEFORE I HAD KIDS
PASS THE FAITH, PLEASE
ALL STRESSED UP AND NO PLACE TO GO
CATCHING CHRISTMAS

Illustrations by TIM CAMPBELL, pp. 1, 2, 3, 4, 5, 6
Illustrations by DANIEL JEFFREY JEWETT pp. 9, 17, 24, 36, 38

THE DEATH OF COMMON SENSE & PROFILES OF THOSE WHO
KNEW HIM © 2012 by Lori Borgman. All rights reserved. Printed
in the United States of America. No part of this book may be used
or reproduced in any manner whatsoever without written permission
except in the case of brief quotations embodied in critical articles and
reviews. For information contact the author at lori@loriborgman.com

FIRST EDITION

Published by:
Good Cheer Publishing
Indianapolis, Indiana

ISBN 978-1-4675-3786-5

Introduction

"The Death of Common Sense" was one of those columns that nearly wrote itself. It was first published in *The Indianapolis Star on* March 15, 1998 and distributed by Knight-Ridder News Service (now McClatchy-Tribune News Service) to newspapers throughout the United States and Canada the following week. At the time, the editor I worked with at the Star said I had written a classic. I thought she was just buttering me up because that particular paper never paid me much, but it turned out she was right.

The essay took on a life of its own. In the ensuing years, I have received my own essay forwarded to me in emails several times a year. Some of the versions had changed a few words here and there, with others attempting to update it, or add their personal touch.

A few years after I'd written it, I Googled the piece out of curiosity and was shocked to see that it had proliferated in cyberspace. It was everywhere on the Internet and nearly always attributed to "Anonymous." I've been called many things as a newspaper columnist, but to be called "Anonymous" hurts the most of all.

I emailed some of the university and professional websites, and even a blogger or two who had used it, identified myself as the author, provided a link to the original publication, and asked for attribution. All of them politely, apologetically, and rather quickly I might add, obliged with the exception of one gentleman. He said he had read the piece long ago and doubted I was the original author. In fact, he accused me of plagiarism. He was accusing me of copying me.

In early 2007, the piece began enjoying a huge

resurgence in popularity. I received multiple requests to reprint it nearly every week - from a high school in Idaho to a yoga magazine in Spain, a real estate networking group and a website for veterinarian techs. I heard from a worker on an oil rig off the Gulf Coast who had read it on the bulletin board of a break room. The Colorado State Penitentiary included it in a newsletter. Banks, insurance companies, and churches posted it on websites and printed it in employee publications. An eighth-grade student in Wisconsin asked to use it in her forensics competition. It was, and still is, popular among radio talk show hosts.

Once in awhile readers would spot it in their local papers with someone else taking credit for it. A man in Cloudcroft, New Mexico, wrote to me about such a situation. I thanked him but said I really didn't have the time to pursue the matter. He wrote back: "hi lori - thanks for your response - the best to you - don't worry ...we'll make sure you get proper attribution - we won't let him get away with it!!!! - bix"

Requests to reprint the essay and inquiries about

how to obtain it in a more permanent form aren't just from people in the States, but from people in Canada, Australia, Great Britain, Scotland and Ireland. A writer in Iceland has translated it into Icelandic and it has also been translated into Greek.

For a brief while, the piece began circulating the Internet attributed to George Carlin. Snopes set the record straight. The only thing worse than being called Anonymous is having your work attributed to someone who is apparently writing from the grave.

For a dead entity, Common Sense has been enjoying a very robust life.

What made the piece so popular? I think it took off because it gave human qualities to an abstract quality that is difficult to define. Try to define common sense in five words or less. It's easier to draw a picture, which is what the essay did.

People knew common sense was dying. They saw it every day in their places of employment, their schools, the media and their neighborhoods. The essay simply put into words what others were already thinking.

As the underpinnings of our great country corrode, like you, I have wondered what can be done. The answer to that question is as individual as we are. For me, part of the answer was to delve further into the life of Common Sense and take a look at those who knew him well: his wife, Discretion; his daughter, Responsibility; his son, Reason; and his step-brothers, Half-Wit and Dim-Wit.

In the same voice "The Death of Common Sense" was written, I have told their stories, too. I hope they make you smile, but above all, I hope they spur you to action. Yes, of course, lament the passing of Common Sense but may his passing also spur you to resolve. Purpose yourself to nurture good character, to live life with intentionality, and to pursue worthy goals. Stand up and speak out. Help protect and preserve the freedom and liberty that has made this nation great.

The Death of Common Sense

Three yards of black fabric enshroud my computer terminal. I am mourning the passing of an old friend by the name of Common Sense. His obituary reads as follows:

Common Sense, aka C.S., lived a long life, but died from heart failure at the brink of the millennium. No one really knows how old he was.

His birth records were long ago entangled in miles and miles of bureaucratic red tape.

Known affectionately to close friends as Horse Sense and Sound Thinking, he selflessly devoted himself to a life of service in homes, schools, hospitals and offices, helping folks get jobs done without a lot of fanfare, whooping and hollering.

Rules and regulations and petty, frivolous lawsuits held no power over C.S. A most reliable sage, he was credited with cultivating the ability to know when to come in out of the rain, the discovery that the early bird gets the worm and how to take the bitter with the sweet.

C.S. developed sound financial policies (don't spend more than you earn), reliable parenting strategies (the adult is in charge, not the kid) and prudent dietary plans (offset eggs and bacon with a little fiber and orange juice).

C.S. was a proud veteran of the Industrial Revolution, the Great Depression, the Technological Revolution and the Smoking Crusades. He survived sundry cultural and educational trends including disco, the men's movement, body piercing, whole language and new math. C.S.'s health began its initial decline in the late 1960s  when he became infected with the If-It-Feels-Good, Do-It virus.

But his waning strength proved no match for the ravages of overbearing federal and state rules and regulations and an oppressive tax code. C.S. was sapped of strength and the will to live as the Ten Commandments became contraband, criminals received better treatment than victims and judges stuck their noses in everything from Boy Scouts to professional baseball and golf.

His deterioration accelerated as schools continued implementing zero-tolerance policies. Reports of 6-year-old boys charged with sexual harassment for kissing classmates, a teen suspended for taking a swig of Scope mouthwash after lunch, girls suspended for possessing Midol and an honor student expelled for having a table

The Death of Common Sense

knife in her school lunch were more than his heart could endure.

As his passing neared, doctors say C.S. drifted in and out of logic but was kept informed of developments regarding regulations on low-flow toilets, mandatory air bags and the coming of CFL light bulbs. Finally, upon hearing about a government plan to ban inhalers from 14 million asthmatics due to a trace of a pollutant that may be harmful to the environment, C.S. breathed his last.

Services will be at Whispering Pines Cemetery.

C.S. was preceded in death by his wife, Discretion. He is survived by his daughter, Responsibility; his son, Reason and two step-brothers, Half-Wit and Dim-Wit.

Memorial contributions may be sent to the Institute for Rational Thought.

Farewell, Common Sense. May you rest in peace.

COMMON SENSE

Fool me once, shame on you;
fool me twice, shame on me.

"Common sense is the knack of seeing things
as they are, and doing things
as they ought to be done."
- Josh Billings

"Philosophy is common sense with big words."
- James Madison

"It is a thousand times better to have common sense
without education than to have education
without common sense."
- Colonel Robert "Bob" Green Ingersoll

Discretion

Common Sense and Discretion shared a long and loving companionship that spanned many years. If there were ever two better-suited shipmates for sailing life's seas, I wish to meet them. C.S. lovingly referred to Discretion as his Sweet Steel Magnolia.

It was Discretion's strong mind that drew Common Sense to her. She was a discerning and sagacious judge of character. Her ability to recognize the truth and goodness of a matter was like a scalpel in the hand of a gifted surgeon.

Discretion had a quiet manner that was reserved and proper, yet charitable and humble. With a silent nod from across the way she would often affirm that Common Sense was headed in the right direction.

She was everyone's favorite confidant and counselor. Secrets were safe with Discretion. She was never one to suffer from loose lips or betray a confidence. The privacy of her friends and family was never for sale. She abhorred public confessions and loathed crocodile tears.

Not one prone to blustering argument, empty blather, or that silly endless stream of consciousness rambling that passes for both literature and conversation these days, Discretion listened first and spoke later. Or often not at all. In the presence of a fool, Discretion would offer a coy smile and whisper, "Give that man enough rope and he'll hang himself."

Discretion was a master of tact and diplomacy. Even with the arrival of electronic communication, Discretion still acknowledged R.S.V.P.s, penned handwritten thank you notes and heartfelt messages of sympathy. She warmly welcomed the stranger, extended hospitality and generally moved with a fluid grace.

She conducted herself with a dignity of days gone by in both speech and conduct. Discretion knew when to turn off her cell phone. She did not send text messages in the midst of a personal conversation or ever scream to someone across a crowded room, "FACEBOOK ME!!"

Discretion had a firm grasp on the appropriate and inappropriate. She grieved at the sexualization of little girls and pole dancing kits on sale at Christmas for adolescents. Raunchy, bawdy and tacky were never her style. Discretion wore pearls, not Mardi Gras beads.

Many were unaware that it was in honor of her high standards that the television industry instituted the caution in the upper left-hand corner of the screen reading, "Viewer discretion advised."

Above all, Discretion was savvy. She played her cards close to her chest. She held her friends close and her enemies closer.

She was fond of saying, "If it sounds too good

to be true, it is," and "There's no such thing as a free lunch." She often admonished others, "If you don't want a matter repeated, don't tell it in the first place."

Once asked to comment on Discretion's remarkable record of sound decision making, her sister Prudence mused, "Discretion was never one to be misled by pleasure."

Shortly before her demise, Discretion began experiencing bouts of nausea precipitated by the public worship of vamps and scalawags who were famous simply for being famous. She was heartbroken by adults who could not grasp the value of entering into adulthood and instead suspended themselves in an endless adolescence.

Nausea mushroomed into full-fledged bleeding ulcers as the masses, unable to think soundly or exercise discernment themselves, sold their liberties, freedoms and very souls to the cadence of smooth talkers in expensive suits and Italian leather shoes.

The end abruptly came when Discretion was waiting for her car to be serviced. She was sitting in the automotive waiting room where the television was turned to one of those daytime talk shows. The audience was screaming and shouting at the guests and the guests were throwing punches at one another. After witnessing three cat fights between well-endowed and scantily-clad women over who the baby daddies of their children were, Discretion gasped, "Culture is dead." She toppled forward and fell face down next to a display of BOOM-BOOM car stereo amplifiers.

It was an unseemly end for a character long known for dignity and good taste.

A private service was held for family members and close friends. No media coverage was allowed and no display of mass hysteria was encouraged. With the exception of one shirt-tail relation who was so obtuse as to wear a T-shirt and flip flops to the memorial, it was a service marked by decorum.

DISCRETION

"Nothing is more dangerous than a friend without discretion; even a prudent enemy is preferable."

- Jean de La Fontaine

"Certainly, it is a world of scarcity. But the scarcity is not confined to iron ore and arable land. The most constricting scarcities are those of character and personality."

-William R. Allen

The better part of valor is discretion;"

- Shakespeare, Henry IV

"A man's discretion makes him slow to anger, And it is his glory to overlook a transgression."

-Proverbs 19:11

Responsibility

As a young child, Responsibility once used her water-color set to paint what she thought was a fine-looking horse (although it was sway back and only had three legs) on her bedroom wall. When asked about the painting on the wall, Responsibility, with paint on her hands and guilt on her face, looked squarely at her mother and father and said her brother did it.

Responsibility's father and mother, Common Sense and Discretion, sat the child down and said, "You're not the sharpest knife in the drawer, but we think we can work with you."

And work they did. They assigned household chores to the child and inspected them. If the chores weren't done properly, Responsibility was made to do them until they were done properly. Responsibility learned to put her dirty dishes in the dishwasher, to take out the trash when it was full, and that work came before play.

"You reap what you sow," her mother often said. "If you don't work, you don't eat," her mother chirped. In a certain light, Responsibility thought that her mother sometimes bore a striking similarity to the Little Red Hen.

In addition to being taught to exercise the small courtesies of saying "please" and "thank you" and "excuse me," Responsibility also learned to say, "I'm the one who made this mess and I'm the one who will clean it up."

Responsibility enjoyed a pleasant childhood and played the usual games children played—Life, Monopoly, Hearts and Crazy Eights, but never the Blame Game or 101 Excuses.

The dog never ate Responsibility's homework, she never accidentally put merchandise in her purse without paying for it at the mall, and her alarm clock never failed to ring.

Responsibility learned that the things that were *expected* were as important as the things that were *inspected*. And that small things were as important as big things.

For want of a nail, a shoe was lost,
For want of a shoe, a horse was lost,
For want of a horse, a battle was lost,
For want of a battle, a kingdom was lost.

Responsibility matured and grew and came to embody a can-do attitude and cheerful optimism. Her sense of responsibility to God, country and fellow man sprang from a deep well of gratitude. Responsibility was thankful for the gift of life, for limbs that worked, a mind that could think, a heart that could love, eyes that could see and ears that could hear. She mercifully cared for those suffering misfortunes and tenderly lent a hand to those in need.

Responsibility entered adulthood entirely capable of managing her own affairs—her finances, her housing, her transportation, and social calendar—all of which has made life increasingly puzzling for Responsibility. She was bewildered by those who took no interest in tending to their own needs or future.

Responsibility positively reeled when others committed awful, sometimes purposeful and egregious offenses without apologizing or making restitution, instead blaming an overactive libido, a night of binge drinking, or a nebulous malaise named stress. "Nobody takes responsibility for themselves anymore," she once quipped. "They just go into therapy."

To this day, Responsibility is still dumbfounded by parents who expect the schools to feed, teach, raise and discipline their children. She is bewildered when adults assume tantrum position, plant their feet on the ground, their hands on their hips and scream, "We're entitled!"

"They don't just want a chicken in every pot," she says, brow furrowed. "They want a gas range for the pot and a side-by-side refrigerator and freezer as well. They want free health care, childcare, retirement benefits, smoke detectors, and cable converter boxes. They want their student loans forgiven, credit card debt erased and the right to live in houses they can't afford.

"The real clincher is," she says, inhaling deeply, "they're willing to yield it all—freedom, liberty, property rights, their wages and profits, even their parental rights—in order to have it all. Was there ever a more willing group of indentured servants?"

Responsibility recently seized a live microphone at a panel discussion on the future of the nation and yelled, "DOESN'T ANYBODY WANT TO TAKE CARE OF

THEMSELVES ANYMORE? WHERE HAVE ALL THE GROWNUPS GONE?" Her hair was hanging in her face, her clothes were disheveled, she had bags under her eyes and the smell of stale coffee on her breath. Responsibility was beside herself.

Responsibility was a train wreck.

She slipped away and composed herself, but the truth is Responsibility often feels a bit daunted these days. But then the winds shift. She travels to one of those small self-reliant corners of the country where harsh weather breeds proud, resourceful, and resolute people. These are the folks that can lift their own sandbags when flood waters lap the river bank. They are the ones that fire up chainsaws after a tornado has carved a path through town. They pull their neighbors from beneath the rubble without first phoning a bureaucrat or waiting for approval from a government agency.

She enjoys observing the entrepreneurs and small businesses determined to press forward. She takes note of parents intentionally raising their families, going against the currents of culture. Responsibility smiles at the houses of worship where the faithful meet and spill into the communities. Her posture straightens as she surveys the non-profits and urban ministries supported solely by private citizens and private donations, and exhales a heavy sigh.

She may totter on occasion, but Responsibility always regains her footing. At her core, Responsibility is robust and Reaganesque.

Responsibility believes in the shining city atop a hill. Responsibility holds fast to the promise of life, liberty and the pursuit of happiness. She knows that responsibility is what yields rights, and that rights without responsibility yield weak minds, and that weak minds make a people vulnerable to tyranny.

Responsibility has a clear vision and strong hope for the future. She also has a snow shovel in the garage, jumper cables in the trunk, canned goods on hand in the pantry and cash in the freezer for unexpected emergencies.

RESPONSIBILITY

"Responsibility is the price of greatness."

-Winston Churchill

"We make men without chests and
expect of them virtue and enterprise.
We laugh at honor and are shocked
to find traitors in our midst.
We castrate and bid the geldings be fruitful."

- C.S. Lewis

"You are not only responsible for what you say,
but also for what you do not say."

- Martin Luther

"Liberty means responsibility.
That is why most men dread it."

- George Bernard Shaw

"I mean to live my life an obedient man, but obedient to
God, subservient to the wisdom of my ancestors; never
to the authority of political truths arrived
at yesterday at the voting booth."

- William F. Buckley, Jr.

"People think responsibility is hard to bear. It's not.
I think that sometimes it is the absence of responsibility
that is harder to bear. You have a great
feeling of impotence."

-Henry Kissinger

I do not know anyone who has got to the top without
hard work. That is the recipe. It will not always get you
to the top, but should get you pretty near.

- Margaret Thatcher

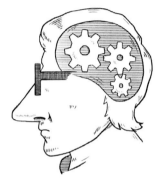

Reason

Reason was always known as the "smarts" in the family.

He wore out his first library card before he turned six and was one of the few in his swim class not to challenge the sign that said, "No running."

Astute - that's what the boy was. Even now he is a voracious reader and keen thinker. This is not to say he always has his nose in a book. On the contrary, he often simply sits and studies the world about him.

Some eat chocolate for pleasure. Reason cogitates.

Many credit Reason with coining the adage, "Think before you speak." The world will never know how many marriages were saved with that one adage alone. Men learned to pause before answering, "Do you like my hair?" "Do these jeans make my backside look big?"

Reason was the one who encouraged people to consider if there was not a Designer behind the design. He nudged people to question the cause of creation and the miracle of birth, to ask where conscience comes from and by what means we are absolved from guilt, and why we all possess an intrinsic yearning to know God.

For many years Reason was at home in the universities, discussing abstract matters with students, posing hypotheses and testing suppositions. He relished teaching how to build a sound argument and spot a fallacious one. Reason especially delighted teaching the fallacies because examples in the media abounded. "Like shooting fish in a barrel!" he howled. His protégés dismantled beer commercials, emotionally driven editorials and poorly reasoned policy with lightning speed.

And then one day Reason asked a class to write a definition of an argumentum ad hominem. Half of them wrote out the recipe for hummus. The entire nation's attention span was shrinking. Students were no longer interested in thinking abstractly or reasoning logically. Reading had become a loathsome chore. Students preferred tapping on cell phones, using apps to find the best price on shoes, or read the menu at the newest Italian restaurant.

One day, Reason's replacements, Feelings and Passion, appeared at his office door with a cardboard box. They waited, noses in the air, disdain oozing from every pore, while Reason packed his belongings. They told him they were sorry this was how it had to be, then escorted him out of the building giving him a slight shove through the final door.

Reason regrouped, assessed his skills in light of the marketplace, and briefly tried "reinventing himself" as they say. Reason tried a stint as a commentator on cable news shows, but it didn't last long. Reason didn't perform well in a live medium. He paused too much, thought too long, and created an awkward silence. He never got the knack of interrupting, rattling off canned talking points or yelling over the other panelists. Truthfully, his fellow commentators ate him for lunch.

Today, Reason does some solo interviews once in awhile with a select few, but largely spends days in his study.

Reason enjoys working alone. It allows him to be slow and methodical. Thorough. Meticulous. It's not that he doesn't know what they say behind his back. "Why does the man waste so much time thinking? If he wants to know something, why doesn't he just Google it?"

"Ah yes," Reason chuckles, "the scholars that read headlines, skim copy and think a sound bite suffices as in-depth analysis."

Reason relishes digging deep, pondering and ruminating. He teases the details out of the big picture and considers the consequences short term and long. He has traveled wide and lived long, giving him a needed perspective others often lack.

The shrinking attention span of the nation still concerns Reason, but does not surprise him. Such is the result of generations who began building a knowledge base with 20-second segments of "educational television" and never graduated beyond the quick cuts of music videos.

Privately, Reason sometimes refers to the shallow segments of the population as the Platte People. This is a reference to the Platte River that crosses from Nebraska into Colorado and is known for being a mile wide and an inch deep. One wit once said the Platte would be a considerable river—if it were turned on edge.

When Reason is on edge, he positively thunders, pacing in his study, hurling rhetorical questions at the walls and bookshelves: "Is there any greater affront than capable people unwilling to think for themselves? How can a democracy without informed citizens survive?"

The window blinds sigh.

"Do the educated feel no duty to the uneducated? If we are not a nation ruled by laws, we will be a nation ruled by men. Have we not learned that deep inside every man is the potential for evil?"

The bookshelves moan.

Reason used to believe that, given a moral and intellectual grounding, mankind was capable of exercising reason and justice and governing himself. These days he wonders. These days Reason also nurses a frequent headache. It is a dull throb, right front. The headaches could be from thinking too hard, or they could be from being surrounded by those who hardly think at all.

REASON

We cannot solve our problems with the same
thinking we used when we created them.

- Albert Einstein

"Reason is the slow and torturous method
by which those who do not
know the truth discover it."

- Blaise Pascal

"Rarely do we find men who willingly engage in hard,
solid thinking. There is an almost universal quest for
easy answers and half-baked solutions. Nothing pains
some people more than having to think.

- Martin Luther King, Jr.

Let our advance worrying
become advance thinking and planning.

- Winston Churchill

"Of all tyrannies, a tyranny sincerely exercised for the good of its victims may be the most oppressive. It would be better to live under robber barons than under omnipotent moral busybodies. The robber baron's cruelty may sometimes sleep, his cupidity may at some point be satiated; but those who torment us for our own good will torment us without end for they do so with the approval of their own conscience."

- C. S. Lewis

"Those who will not reason, are bigots,
those who cannot, are fools,
and those who dare not, are slaves."

- Lord Byron

"In matters of style, swim with the current; in matters of principle, stand like a rock."

- Thomas Jefferson

Half-Wit and Dim-Wit

Half-wit and Dim-Wit were not the names the boys were given at birth. They earned those names in elementary school, where they graduated at the top of their self-esteem class. Of course, all the kids graduated at the top of the class. All the kids received trophies. All the kids received ribbons. All the kids were winners. And all the kids knew it was a joke—all except a few. Half-Wit and Dim-Wit bought it hook, line and sinker. They would skip through the school halls, arms spread wide, singing at the top of their voices:

> *I'm special! I'm special!*
> *I'm special because I'm me.*
> *I'm wonderful and special*
> *I love me, me, me!*

The teachers applauded; the principal beamed.

And then one street-wise kid said to another, "Who are the narcissists?"

"Half-Wit and Dim-Wit," somebody answered.

Half-Wit and Dim-Wit—who believed they really *were* the smartest, most beautiful, most creative, most deserving, marvelous creatures who ever fell to earth— overheard the exchange.

They whirled around and shouted, "We can do anything we want! We can be anything we want! We can go anywhere we want!"

A no-nonsense mother of five passing by said, "The only place you two are going is home. Somebody get these twerps on their bus!"

By middle school, Half-Wit and Dim-Wit were so entrenched in the culture of rights, revisionist history, and moral relativism that they were quite easily, and very often, offended. They became snitches for the ACLU. They filed daily text message reports from restroom stalls: "SOS!! Social studies textbook teaches Manifest Destiny—with NO apology! Health teacher used words husband and wife instead of partners. Send lawyers!"

Half-Wit and Dim-Wit secured court injunctions banning prayer from their high school commencement. They were privately assured that should some valedictorian try to slip God into a speech, said student would be slapped with a hate speech charge and do some serious time.

Half-Wit and Dim-Wit's pictures were side-by-side in the high school yearbook. The caption beneath them read, "Most likely to become malpractice lawyers with cheesy 1-800 number television commercials featuring fake bookshelves in the background."

When they announced they were going to law

school, everyone yawned.

After passing the bar, Dim-Wit took the path of the trial lawyer. He handled some highly publicized cases, including a man who sued his employer because he fell after propping his ladder on the branch he was cutting.

He also represented the man who sued a beer company because he couldn't get the hot looking chicks pictured in the ad, even though he drank the beer. His finest moment, however, was representing a married man who sued a strip club because the stiletto of a woman performing a lap dance hit him in the eye.

Dim-Wit once even represented a prisoner at Guantanamo - pro bono, of course - then turned around and charged his own grandmother an arm and a leg for setting up a living trust.

"Hey, money doesn't grow on trees," Dim-Wit said, as his aging and frail grandmother stuck a For Sale sign in her front yard.

Half-Wit took the path of the policy wonk. He had a natural talent for, verbosity, backroom deals and running paper shredders.

Half-Wit took particular pride crafting legislation for massive government programs with no regard as to where the funding might come from or the devastating tax burden that would be incurred by generations to come.

This is not to say Half-Wit and Dim-Wit always worked independently. Together they have taken courageous stands against trans fats, salt, carbonated beverages, obese people, evangelicals, Catholics, school choice, gun rights, Wal-Mart, God, SUVs, anyone who is pro-life and the Pledge of Allegiance.

That's fine to know what they are against, but what are they for you ask? Plenty! Expanding government, trillion-dollar bailouts, federal takeover of private industry, salary caps, seizing private property, unbridled spending, confiscatory taxes, dismantling the Bill of Rights, rewriting the Constitution, and free universal access to Viagra. Next on their agenda is attempting to enforce a national bedtime.

Both Half-Wit and Dim-Wit have gone completely green, or at least that's what they say publicly. Truth be told, neither of them has recycled an aluminum can in years. And at this very moment, Half-Wit has plans for a 19-bedroom mansion with a roof-top heliport, tennis courts, lap pool and landing strip for his jet. Half-Wit will live alone on the estate. He plans on conserving energy by limiting toilet flushes for his houseguests.

Dim-Wit believes he is saving the planet in larger increments. He was among the first to switch to the

environmentally friendly curlicue CFL light bulbs. He now has a milk jug nearly full of mercury collected from the broken bulbs.

"The little beads are so cute and jiggly," Dim-Wit says. "I think the neighborhood children will love playing with them."

Half-Wit and Dim-Wit both suffer from frequent bouts of affluent guilt and, consequently, love hosting "Give Back Days" in which they browbeat others for not giving more generously to their communities.

Truth be told, the last charitable contribution of any size either of them made was twelve years ago when a homeless man stole Dim-Wit's wallet. But then, Half-Wit and Dim-Wit have always believed that hypocrisy is a virtue.

The important thing is that they maintain good self-esteem. Still special after all these years.

HALF-WIT AND DIM-WIT

If at first you don't succeed, sue somebody.

Do unto others
before they do unto you.

He who laughs last
. . . is probably a little slow.

"People who enjoy
meetings should not be
in charge of anything."

- Thomas Sowell

"Do not put off 'til tomorrow what can be put
off 'til day-after-tomorrow just as well."

- Mark Twain

"Half the harm that is done in this world is due to
people who want to feel important. They don't mean to
do harm—but the harm does not interest them. Or they
do not see it, or they justify it because they are absorbed
in the endless struggle to think well of themselves."

- T. S. Eliot

Afterword

Is Common Sense really dead?

Some have reported seeing a hint of color returning to his face. Others claim they saw a small puff of air blow from his cheeks.

I can almost convince myself that the old sage will rise up and walk—and then I scan the headlines.

In Vermont, a lawmaker sought to legalize teen sexting, the sending and receiving of graphic sexual pictures between kids 18 years old and younger, in order to avoid youthful offenders being listed as sex offenders. An interesting debate. But even more interesting was the "expert in communicating with teens," who commented on the matter. She said parents should talk with their teens about sexting, but not use language saying this is right, or this is wrong. The expert suggested parents use terms like cool and uncool.

We are sorely missing Common Sense when we listen to experts who advise us not to use words like right and wrong. It's just, well, uncool.

If Common Sense did think about making a comeback, he probably thought twice upon hearing of the Pittsburgh-area middle school student suspended after a random search turned up an eyebrow shaver in her handbag. Who knows what treacherous things the girl planned on doing with an eyebrow shaver. Separate the eyebrows of the principal? Trim ear hair on a math teacher?

The school recommended the girl be expelled for the rest of the school year and for 45 days next year. The student is a Girl Scout, a member of the school's basketball team, the choir and the leadership team. The overreaction on the part of the school proves there are some things not even a Girl Scout can be prepared for.

And just when you think there couldn't possibly be one more nail in the coffin of Common Sense, you learn about businesses using government monies intended to create jobs, indeed creating jobs, not here but overseas.

In light of deeply-rooted idiotic policies, the choke-hold of bureaucracy and the ever-present fear of lawsuits, is it possible to resurrect Common Sense?

Absolutely. With a few strategic chest compressions, it is entirely possible.

Our starting point is rebuilding the moral skeleton. We are entrenched in a modern culture that relishes vice—pole-dancing teens, body part humor woven into every sitcom, along with the bleeped obscenities, and the general glorification of skanks and twits. Let's not forget Madonna, old enough to be post-menopausal and a grandmother, entertaining fans by flashing her breast.

We've forgotten what virtue looks like. Virtue looks like vertebrae. Virtue is the backbone of Common

Sense.

In the movie, "The Gladiator," Marcus Aurelius strives to teach his son the four chief virtues: Wisdom, Justice, Fortitude and Temperance. What are the virtues we attempt to teach our children today? Sadly, "Be nice" is often as deep as our character education goes. The ancient Romans had a firm grasp on virtue. They believed virtue was essential to the character development of the individual and of the nation. A few of the virtues they aspired to include:

Tenacity: Strength of mind, the ability to stick to one's purpose.

Mercy: Mildness and gentleness.

Gravity: A sense of the importance of the matter at hand, responsibility and earnestness.

Frugalness: Economy and simplicity of style, without being miserly.
(A revolutionary thought: If you can't afford it, do without and make do with what you have.)

Humor: Ease of manner, courtesy, openness, and friendliness.

Respectability: The image that one presents as a respectable member of society.

Industriousness: Hard work.

Humanity: Refinement, civilization, learning, and being cultured.
(It's OK not to act like a barbarian.)

Our moral backbone has advanced osteoporosis. It's time to step up the calcium. The classical Roman virtues are lofty, but it's time to raise the bar. Meditate on them, reflect on them. Talk about them with your children and grandchildren. Raise the level of the conversation.

Prudence: Foresight, wisdom, and personal discretion.

Wholesomeness: Health and cleanliness.
(This one would prohibit wearing pajama pants to college classes and Wal-Mart.)

Truthfulness: Honesty in dealing with others.

Equity: Fair dealing both within government and among the people.
(This would mean if our incomes go down, the income of our elected leaders shouldn't be going up.)

Justice: As expressed by sensible laws and governance.

Liberality: Generous giving.

Nobility: Noble action in the public sphere.

Endurance, Patience: The ability to weather storms and crisis.

Providence, Forethought: The ability of Roman society to survive trials and manifest a greater destiny.

Courage: Especially of leaders within society and government.

We also need to return to thinking as opposed to feeling. We excel at emoting, sniffling, rationalizing, whining, apologizing and bowing, but we don't do as well when it comes to thinking. Emotion-based decisions make us feel better for the short-term, but they are rarely a solution long-term. Only by clear and sound thinking can we link actions with consequences. Let me repeat that: Actions have consequences. As a man sows, so he reaps. When we finally link actions with consequences, we will be able to see the long-term benefits, or as is often the case today, the eventual peril of our ideas and actions.

If we were able to think clearly today, we would see that much of our country's financial mess has been brought about by repeated quick fixes. Our government's most frequently employed short-term solution: If it doesn't move, throw money at it. If it starts to move, throw more money at it.

Clear thinking also would enable us to see that financial security is inextricably linked with national security. We would stop adding zeroes to our national debt, which seems a heavy burden now, but will become a crushing and crippling burden to future generations.

When we think clearly, we can see that many of the entitlement programs that are meant to ease the way for people do little more than enslave people. There is nothing liberating or dignified about languishing in a state of constant dependence on others.

Clear thinking also allows us to see that it is the nature of government to intrude on the freedoms of its citizens. Thomas Paine, who authored "Common Sense" in 1776, viewed government as a necessary evil. We have put ourselves and our freedoms in jeopardy by viewing government as our sugar daddy and savior.

As it is the nature of government to intrude upon its citizens, so it should be the nature of freedom-loving citizens to resist the intrusion. We have become so accustomed to government intrusion that when another intrusive measure is thrust upon us—*No more Big Gulp sodas for you, New York City!*—we aren't outraged or incensed. We don't cry out in protest that our government treats us like children. We barely shrug.

Healthy democracy is insured solely by citizens who have a deep, abiding love and an iron-fist grip on the importance of liberty, freedom, and self-rule.

Resuscitating Common Sense is critical. Thinking soundly, acting prudently, raising expectations and making our voices heard in the marketplace is not an option.

The future and well-being of our nation depend on it. Freedom and liberty demand it.

The
Death *of*
Common
Sense
And profiles of those
who knew him

available exclusively at
www.loriborgman.com/books

ebook on amazon.com

For quantity discounts, email
books@loriborgman.com